SUPER SPORTS STORIES

BASMA BALANCES ON THE BEAM

by Blake Hoena
illustrated by Christos Skaltsas

GRASSHOPPER

Tools for Parents & Teachers

Grasshopper Books enhance imagination and introduce the earliest readers to fiction with fun storylines and illustrations. The easy-to-read text supports early reading experiences with repetitive sentence patterns and sight words.

Before Reading

- Discuss the cover illustration. What do readers see?
- Look at the glossary together. Discuss the words.

Read the Book

- Read the book to the child, or have him or her read independently.
- "Walk" through the book and look at the illustrations. Who is the main character? What is happening in the story?

After Reading

- Prompt the child to think more. Ask: Basma injured her ankle and had to take a break from gymnastics. Why do you think this makes her nervous when she returns?

Grasshopper Books are published by Jump!
5357 Penn Avenue South
Minneapolis, MN 55419
www.jumplibrary.com

Library of Congress Cataloging-in-Publication Data

Names: Hoena, B. A., author.
Skaltsas, Christos, illustrator.
Title: Basma balances on the beam / by Blake Hoena;
illustrated by Christos Skaltsas.
Description: Minneapolis, MN: Jump!, Inc., [2024]
Series: Super sports stories | Includes index.
Audience: Ages 7-10.
Identifiers: LCCN 2022048368 (print)
LCCN 2022048369 (ebook)
ISBN 9798885243797 (hardcover)
ISBN 9798885243803 (paperback)
ISBN 9798885243810 (ebook)
Subjects: CYAC: Self-Confidence–Fiction.
Gymnastics–Fiction. | LCGFT: Sports fiction.
Readers (Publications)
Classification: LCC PZ7.H67127 Bav 2024 (print)
LCC PZ7.H67127 (ebook)
DDC [Fic] –dc23
LC record available at https://lccn.loc.gov/2022048368
LC ebook record available at https://lccn.loc.gov/2022048369

Editor: Eliza Leahy
Direction and Layout: Anna Peterson
Illustrator: Christos Skaltsas

Printed in the United States of America at
Corporate Graphics in North Mankato, Minnesota.

Table of Contents

Bouncing Back

As Basma walks into the gymnasium, she hears her friend Ting cheer. "Basma is back!"

"Coach Leigh said you'd be at this meet!" Eve says.

"How is your ankle sprain?" Ting asks as the teammates stretch.

"It feels better," Basma says. "But the doctor said I should tape it to be safe."

"You're ready to get back on the balance beam!" Eve says.

I hope so, Basma thinks. The beam is her favorite event—or it was before she fell off and sprained her ankle a few weeks ago.

“Today we start on the balance beam,” says Coach Leigh. “Let’s do some warm-ups. Basma, you’re up.”

Basma takes a deep breath. *I can do this*, she tells herself.

But as she prepares to mount the beam, she feels nervous. *What if I fall again?* she worries. She places a shaky hand on the beam.

"You've got this, Basma!" Ting shouts.

Basma lifts herself onto the beam. She kicks one leg over and then lifts her legs into a v-sit.

Then, she quickly kicks her legs backward. Placing both hands on the beam, she presses into a handstand.

Basma points one foot forward and one backward. She arches her back and places her back foot on the beam. But as she rises to a standing position, she loses her balance.

Oh no! Basma thinks.

She falls off the beam and lands on the mat below.

"Is your ankle OK?" Eve asks.

"It's fine," Basma grumbles.

But why is this so hard? she wonders. *I've done this routine hundreds of times.*

"You're just shaking the dust off, Basma," Coach says. "Don't give up!"

After warm-ups, it's time for the meet to begin! Basma gets back on the balance beam.

She mounts into a v-sit and quickly presses into a handstand. Then she arches her back and places her feet on the beam to return to a standing position.

Basma feels her confidence coming back.
I can do this! she tells herself.

She launches into a split jump.

Thump! She sticks the landing.

She does a spin.

After a few more moves, Basma prepares for her dismount. She does a front tuck off the end of the beam. She sticks the landing!

Her coach and team clap and cheer.

"I'm back!" Basma says.

Let's Review!

Basma performs on the balance beam. There are four official women's gymnastics events. Take a look!

balance beam: Gymnasts perform a routine on a beam that is 16.5 feet (5 meters) long and 4 inches (10 centimeters) wide.

uneven bars: Gymnasts perform a routine on two bars at different heights.

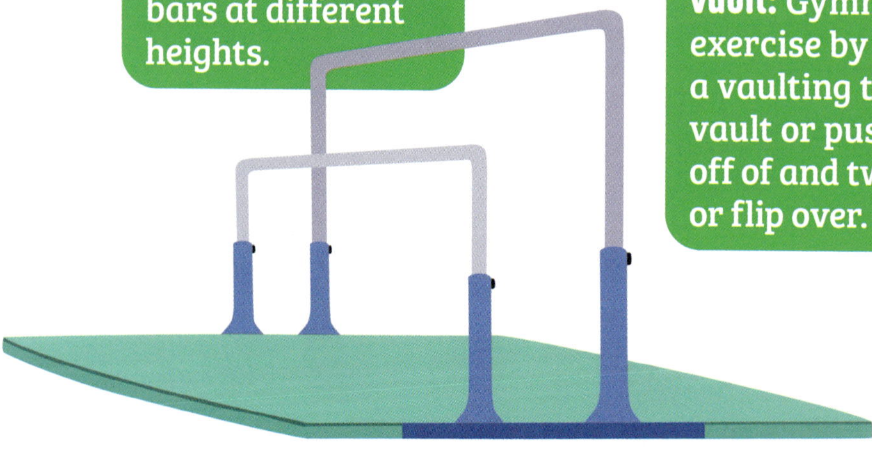

vault: Gymnasts perform an exercise by running toward a vaulting table that they vault or push off of and twist or flip over.

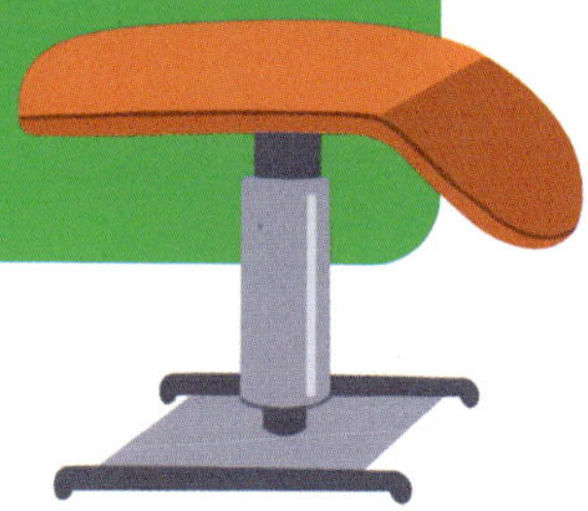

floor: Gymnasts perform a routine on an open, flat area. They mix dance moves and tumbling.

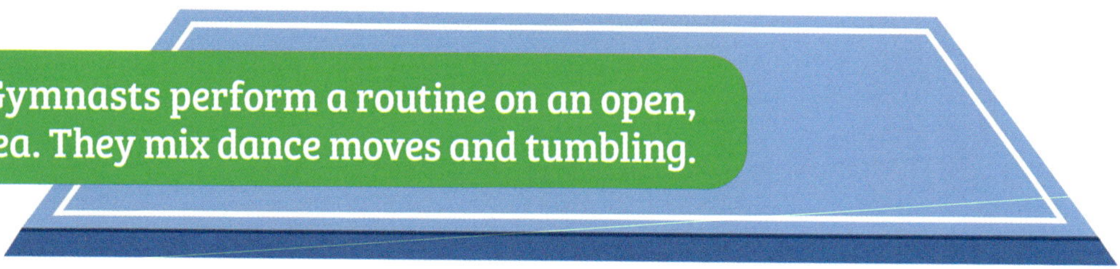

Gymnastics Equipment

What equipment does Basma need to do a balance beam routine? Take a look!

To Learn More

Finding more information is as easy as 1, 2, 3.

1. Go to www.factsurfer.com
2. Enter "**Basmabalancesonthebeam**" into the search box.
3. Choose your book to see a list of websites.

Glossary

confidence: A belief that you have the necessary ability to succeed.

dismount: A move in which a gymnast leaps off an apparatus, such as a balance beam.

front tuck: A forward flip in which a gymnast tucks their knees toward their chest.

meet: A gymnastics competition in which gymnasts compete in four events.

mount: A move in which a gymnast gets on an apparatus.

routine: A series of moves that are done as part of a performance.

split jump: A split performed while jumping in the air.

sprain: To twist a joint, such as an ankle, causing an injury.

v-sit: A seated position in which a gymnast lifts their legs in such a way that their body forms a V shape.

warm-ups: A set of exercises done to get ready to compete.

Index